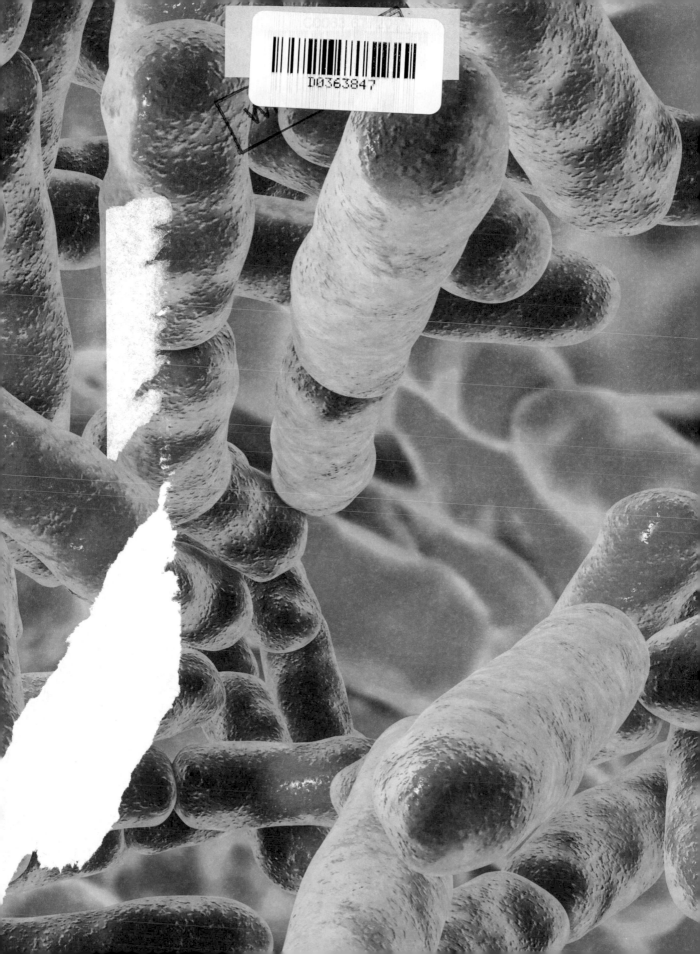

SCIENCE IS EVERYWHERE

OUR LIVING PLANET

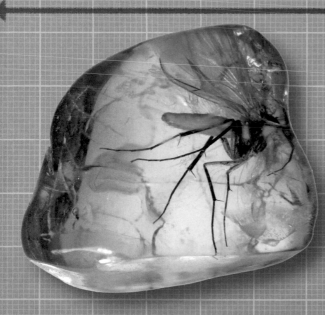

Life and evolution on Earth

Rob Colson

WAYLAND

First published in Great Britain
in 2018 by Wayland
Copyright © Hodder and Stoughton, 2018

Wayland
An imprint of Hachette
Children's Group
Part of Hodder and Stoughton
Carmelite House
50 Victoria Embankment
London EC4Y 0DZ

Executive editor: Adrian Cole
Produced by Tall Tree Ltd
Written by: Rob Colson
Designer: Ben Ruocco

ISBN: 978 1 5263 0504 6
10 9 8 7 6 5 4 3 2 1

An Hachette UK Company
www.hachette.co.uk
www.hachettechildrens.co.uk

Printed and bound in China

The website addresses (URLs) included
in this book were valid at the time of
going to press. However, it is possible
that contents or addresses may have
changed since the publication of this book.
No responsibility for any such changes
can be accepted by either the author or
the Publisher.

t-top, b-bottom, l-left, r-right, c-centre,
front cover-fc, back cover-bc
All images courtesy of Dreamstime.com,
unless indicated:
Inside front Kateryna Kon; fc, bc
Pablo631; fctr Mavrl; fctl Orionmystery;
fcbr Seanstudio; fcb Ogmaassociates;
fcbl Zhengzaishanchu; bctr, 26bl Tvphoto;
bctl, 20 Dslrpix; bccr Isselee; 1bl, 27cl
Likrista82; 4br OAR/National Undersea
Research Program/NOAA; 4-5t NASA;
5tr Zepherwind; 5c Vectorlibellule;
5br Pixelchaos; 6l Dibrova; 6br, Photka;
8c Eknarin Maphichai; 8bc Aona2303;
9tl Salparadis; 9tr Creative Commons
Attribution-Share Alike 3.0 Unported;
10c Nattaya Makerd; 11bl Mazzzur;
11tr Supereagle; 11cr Wpehlemann;
12bl shutterstock/24Novembers;
12-13t, 29br shutterstock/Dmitry375;
13tr Johncox1958; 13bl Jfikar;
13br Red2000; 14cr Mmariomm;
14br shutterstock/Videopoint; 14bl
Fedor Labyntsev; 15t shutterstock/
BlueRingMedia; 15bl shutterstock/
Naoto Shinkai; 15br Astrid228; 16tr,
26c, 29br Mexrix; 16-17b Korovin;
17tr, 31tr Taratata; 17bl Creative
Commons Attribution 2.0 Generic (CC
BY 2.0); 18cl Silksatsunrise; 18cr
Varfolomeija; 19tr julianwphoto; 19cr
Simoneemanphotography; 19bl Sablin;
19br Dennisvdwater; 19b Whitcomberd;
21cr Kellyplz; 21bl Elena Kozyreva;
22 Satori13; 23tr shutterstock/
Kateryna Kon; 23cl Creative Commons
Attribution-Share Alike 3.0 Unported;
23br Macrovector; 24b Sloth92; 25t
Iadarob; 25cl J.A. Siderius; 26cr NASA;
27tr Creative Commons Attribution 2.0
Generic (CC BY 2.0); 27br shutterstock/
Handoko Ramawidjaya Bumi; 28b
Edolzan; 29tl Yulan; 29cr Freebilly; 29br
Robisklp; 30tr Viter8; 30cr LinaTruman;
30bl Likrista82; 32t Stylephotographs

Every attempt has been made to
clear copyright. Should there be any
inadvertent omission please apply to the
publisher for rectification.

Contents

The Blue Marble

Our planet Earth is the only place in the Universe that we know to support life.

Known as The Blue Marble, this photograph of Earth was taken in 1972 from the space craft **Apollo 17**. Conditions on Earth are just right for life to exist:

- **Water is plentiful**. Water forms **more than half** of the material in all living things.

- Most of the planet is above 0°C but below 100°C, meaning that water can exist in **liquid form**.

- Light from the Sun provides a **source of energy**.

- The atmosphere contains the gases **oxygen, carbon dioxide** and **nitrogen**, all of which are essential for building and maintaining life.

Early life forms appeared on Earth more than **4 billion years ago**. The first life may have been **tiny microbes that lived by hot hydrothermal vents** at the bottom of the oceans. These are cracks in Earth's crust through which hot, mineral-rich water leaks.

Life in the oceans

Scientists believe that comb jellies may have been the first animals on Earth. Fossils of comb jellies have been found that are

550 million years old.

"Can I come home now?"

Moving onto land

Life appeared on land about **500 million years ago**. The first life on land may have been tiny fungi. When they rotted, the fungi **helped to create soil** for plants such as mosses to take root. **The first dinosaurs appeared 230 million years ago.** Modern humans appeared just **200,000 years** ago.

Evolution

Different forms of life, called species, have developed through a process called evolution.

Giraffes have evolved long necks to reach high leaves.

Species

A species is a group of **similar organisms** that reproduce with one another. The members of a species that are best adapted to survive produce many offspring and pass their abilities on to those offspring. This process is called **natural selection**, and over time it leads to the appearance of new species with new abilities. All life has evolved from a common ancestor in the distant past.

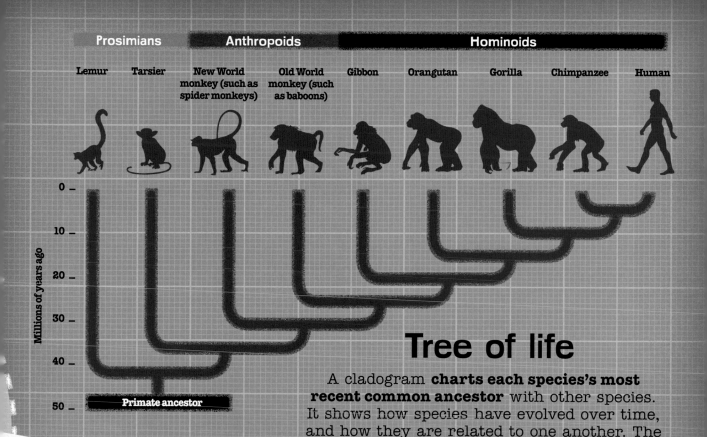

Prosimians		Anthropoids		Hominoids				
Lemur	Tarsier	New World monkey (such as spider monkeys)	Old World monkey (such as baboons)	Gibbon	Orangutan	Gorilla	Chimpanzee	Human

Millions of years ago

0 —

10 —

20 —

30 —

40 —

50 —

Primate ancestor

Tree of life

A cladogram **charts each species's most recent common ancestor** with other species. It shows how species have evolved over time, and how they are related to one another. The cladogram, above, shows how primates are related to one another.

Darwin's finches

Green warbler finch – narrow bill for probing and catching insects

Small tree-finch – short, curved bill for catching insects and biting through tree bark

Medium ground-finch – thick bill for crushing small seeds

Large ground-finch – powerful bill for cracking nuts

The English naturalist **Charles Darwin** was the first person to propose that new species appeared through evolution. During a trip around the world in the 1830s, Darwin studied the finches on the **Galápagos Islands** in the Pacific. He realised that species of finch on different islands had

evolved different bills

over time to suit their diets.

Living off the Sun

Plants take the energy they need to live and grow from the Sun. They do this using a process called photosynthesis.

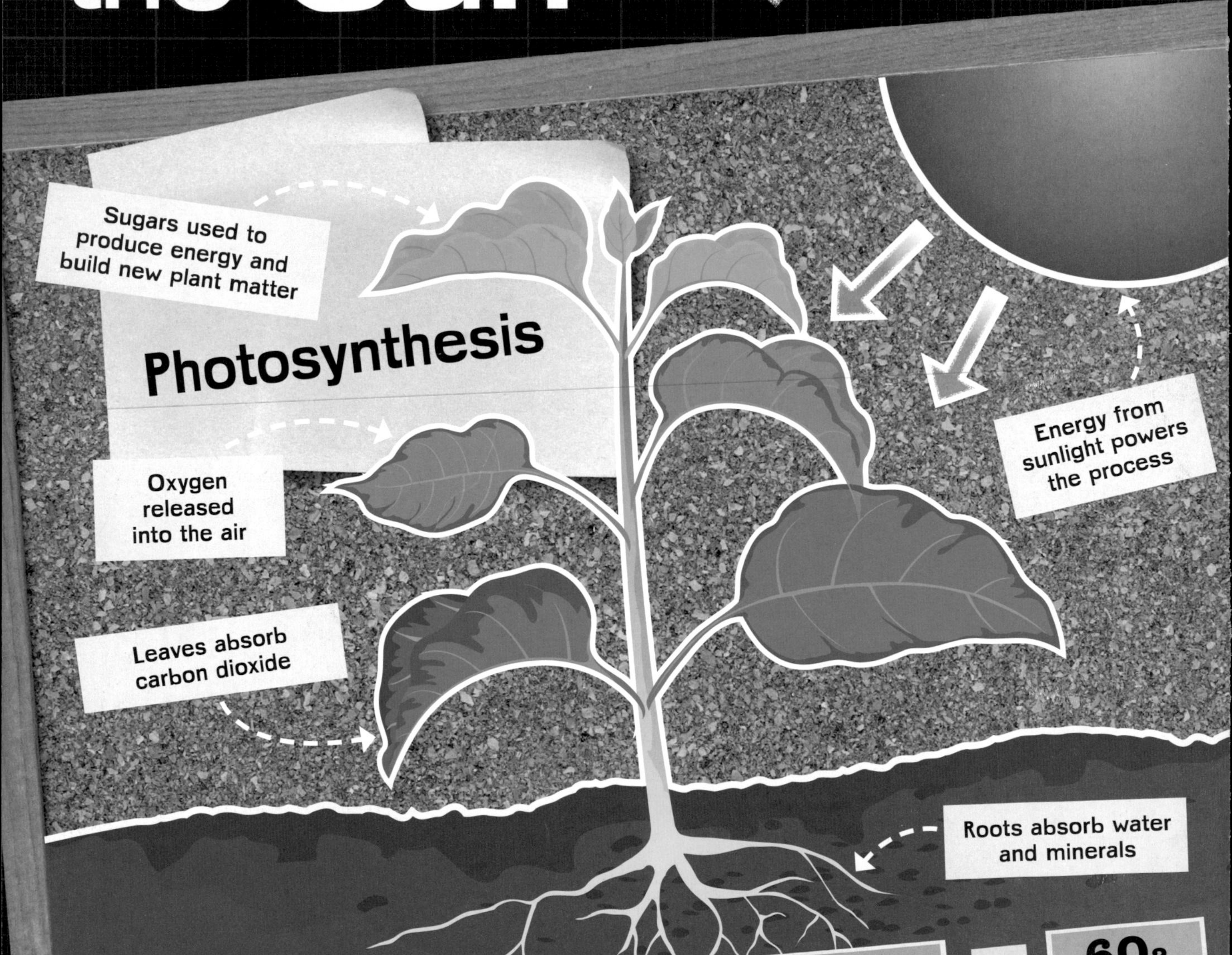

Sugars used to produce energy and build new plant matter

Photosynthesis

Oxygen released into the air

Energy from sunlight powers the process

Leaves absorb carbon dioxide

Roots absorb water and minerals

$$6CO_2 + 6H_2O = C_6H_{12}O_6 + 6O_2$$

6CO₂ Carbon dioxide

6H₂0 Water

C₆H₁₂O₆ Sugars

6O₂ Oxygen

The oxygen we breathe

About half the photosynthesis in the world is carried out by **trees and plants on land**. The other half is carried out by **tiny algae in the oceans**. The process releases oxygen into the atmosphere. Living things need oxygen for an energy-producing process called

respiration,

which uses oxygen and produces carbon dioxide. Without plants and algae to replenish the stocks, all the oxygen in the atmosphere would be used up in just a few hundred years.

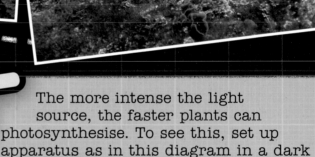

TRY THIS

The more intense the light source, the faster plants can photosynthesise. To see this, set up apparatus as in this diagram in a dark room. First place the lamp **10 cm** from the pondweed. Leave for **five minutes** then come back and count the **number of bubbles** the pondweed produces in a minute. Move the lamp back by **10 cm** and repeat, then move it back again at 10 cm intervals **up to 50 cm**. The bubbles from the pondweed are oxygen produced by photosynthesis. **How does the distance of the lamp affect the amount of oxygen the pondweed produces?**

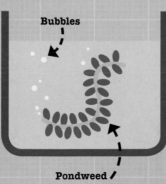

Bubbles

Pondweed

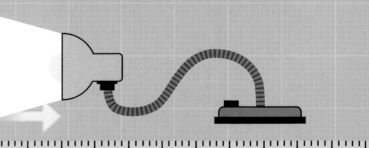

10   20   30   40   50

Flowering plants

Many plants make flowers in order to reproduce. Most flowers produce eggs and sperm. The eggs need to be fertilised by the sperm of a different flower (of the same species) to produce a seed that will grow into a new plant.

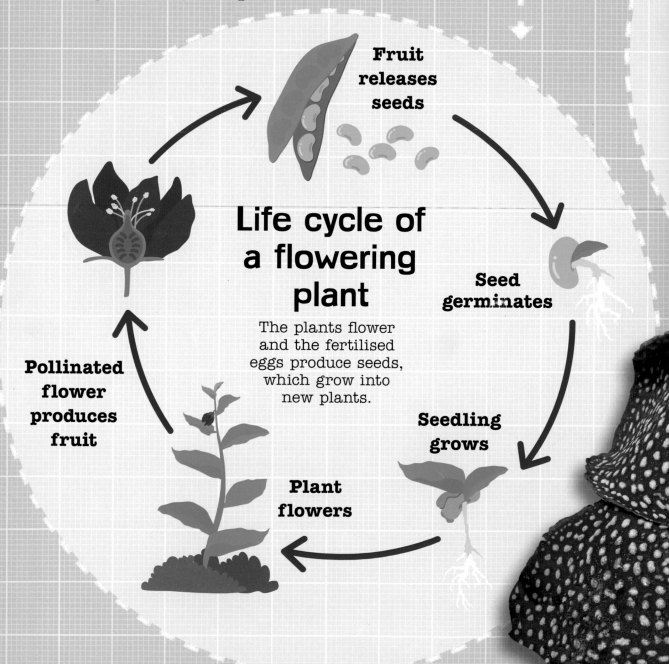

Fruit releases seeds

Life cycle of a flowering plant

The plants flower and the fertilised eggs produce seeds, which grow into new plants.

Seed germinates

Seedling grows

Plant flowers

Pollinated flower produces fruit

Pollinators

To make a fertilised seed, most flowers need to send **sperm-containing pollen** from one plant to another. As plants cannot move, they need help to do this.
Wind-pollinated flowers such as those of grasses are small and drab-looking. The pollen is produced in huge quantities to be carried away by the wind. By chance, some of it will reach another flower.
Insect-pollinated flowers make a lot of effort **to attract animals such as bees**. They are often large and colourful and contain a **sugary nectar** to reward the animals for visiting. The pollen is sticky so that it sticks to the bodies of the animals as they

drink the nectar.

The animals carry the pollen to the next flower, where it fertilises the eggs.

Juicy fruit

Once they have been pollinated, many plants make fruits, which are eaten by animals. The seeds pass through the animals to be left on the ground in their stools and grow into a new plant.

The Indonesian plant
Rafflesia arnoldii
makes the largest flowers in the world. Its flowers are about 1 metre in diameter and smell of rotting flesh. This smell is horrible to us, but very attractive to the flies that pollinate the plant.

Animals with a backbone

Vertebrates are animals with a backbone. They include mammals, reptiles, birds, amphibians and fish. Vertebrates such as reptiles and amphibians are ectothermic, or cold-blooded. This means that their body temperature changes depending on their surroundings. Other vertebrates such as mammals and birds are endothermic, or warm-blooded. They keep their body temperature steady at all times.

Reptiles

Reptiles such as **snakes**, **lizards** and **crocodiles** have scaly skin and lay soft, leathery eggs. Some reptiles, such as **turtles**, spend most of their lives in water, but the females must return to land to lay their eggs.

Vertebrae

"Brrrrr I'm cold."

This is the skeleton of a tiger. A series of bones called vertebrae run from the tiger's **neck down its back** to its tail to form a vertebral column. Inside this is a bundle of nerves called the **spinal cord,** which carries signals between the brain and the rest of the body.

Mammals

Humans belong to a group of vertebrates called mammals. Mammals have **hairy bodies** and the females produce milk to feed their young. Most mammals give birth to **live young** rather than laying eggs.

Macaque mothers carry their babies for their first few weeks of life.

Vertebrate animals

Amphibians

Amphibians, such as **frogs** and **newts** are vertebrates that spend some time in water and some time on land. The young have gills and live underwater. The adults have lungs and can breathe air. The young of frogs are called tadpoles. They develop in water before emerging onto the land as miniature froglets.

Tadpole

Tadpole with legs developing

Adult frog

Poison dart frogs protect themselves with toxic skin.

TRY THIS

As mammals, humans are **warm-blooded**. To test your temperature, place the tip of a thermometer under your armpit for about 30 seconds. Your temperature varies a little, but when you're healthy, the temperature under your armpit stays between 35.9 and 36.7°C. With an adult's help, clean the thermometer and take the temperature under your tongue. It should be about 0.5°C higher.

Creepy crawlies

Insects and spiders are small animals that do not have a backbone. Their skeletons are on the outside of their bodies.

Exoskeletons

A spider's body is covered with a hard exoskeleton. As it grows, the spider must replace its exoskeleton with a new one. It does this by

moulting.

A new skeleton forms under the old one, and the spider then **crawls out of its old skin**. A spider is very vulnerable when it moults, as the new exoskeleton takes time to harden.

Jumping spider exoskeleton after a moult

Spinning a web

Spiders make a substance called silk in organs called spinnerets. Silk is strong and flexible and many spiders use it to spin webs to catch prey.

Orb-weaving spiders weave circular webs. Unsuspecting prey such as insects fly into the webs and get stuck.

Transforming shapes

Butterflies are insects whose bodies undergo huge changes as they develop from egg to adult.

1. Butterflies lay their eggs on leaves.

2. The eggs hatch into larvae called caterpillars, which feed on the leaves and grow quickly.

3. When they are fully grown, the caterpillars form a pupa, or chrysalis.

4. Inside the pupa, a remarkable change called metamorphosis takes place, as the short, stubby caterpillar grows wings to emerge as an adult butterfly.

Dragonflies are insects that lay their eggs underwater. The eggs hatch into larvae called **nymphs**, which are underwater predators that hunt tadpoles and small fish. When they are fully grown, the nymphs emerge from the water, shed their skin and fly off as adult dragonflies.

Funnel-web spiders line their burrows with silk. They lay 'trip lines' that alert them to the presence of prey.

Tangle web spiders make irregular tangled webs to catch prey.

15

Ocean life

About 71 per cent of the surface of Earth is covered in water. A huge variety of life forms are found in the oceans. Like land animals, ocean animals need oxygen to survive. Ocean mammals come to the surface to breathe. Fish take in oxygen that is dissolved in the water.

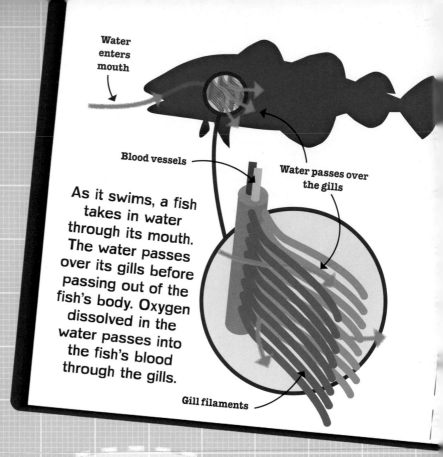

Water enters mouth

Blood vessels

Water passes over the gills

As it swims, a fish takes in water through its mouth. The water passes over its gills before passing out of the fish's body. Oxygen dissolved in the water passes into the fish's blood through the gills.

Gill filaments

Coral reefs

Coral reefs are found in warm tropical oceans. They occupy much less than **1 per cent of the ocean floor**, but about

a quarter of all ocean species

live there. Reefs form in shallow water, often creating islands and lagoons.

Ocean mammals

Whales and dolphins are mammals whose ancestors returned to the oceans about 50 million years ago. They live their whole lives in the ocean, but must come to the surface regularly to breathe. They do not breathe through their mouths but through

blowholes

at the top of their heads.

The beluga whale lives in the Arctic Ocean, feeding on fish, squid, octopus, crab and snails. Its white skin camouflages it against the polar ice.

Coral reefs are built up by tiny animals called **polyps**, which live on the surface of the coral. When they die, the polyps' skeletons become hard and new polyps **grow on top of them**. The Great Barrier Reef, off the east coast of Australia, is the world's largest coral reef.

More than 1,500 species

of fish live there. Hiding in the crevices on the look out for a meal are giant moray eels, which can grow up to **3 metres long**. However, one tiny fish fearlessly seeks out the moray eel. The **cleaner wrasse** eats parasites on the eel's skin. In return, the eel offers the tiny wrasse protection.

"Don't worry, I'm OK."

The **hunters** and the **hunted**

Animals that eat other animals are called predators. The animals that they eat are called prey. Predators are often fast and have fearsome weapons, while prey animals have evolved ways to avoid becoming a meal.

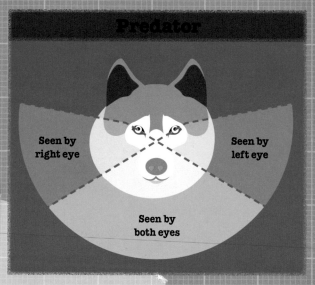

Predator

Seen by right eye

Seen by left eye

Seen by both eyes

Keeping an eye out

Predators often have two eyes at **the front of their faces.**

This gives them good judgement of distance when they pounce on their prey as they can see it with both eyes. Prey animals often have eyes on the sides of their faces. This gives them an all-round view to spot predators sneaking up on them.

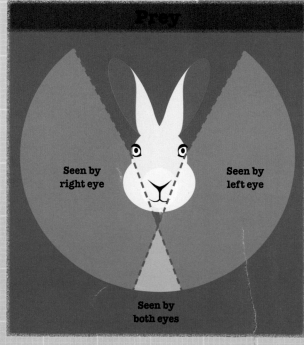

Prey

Seen by right eye

Seen by left eye

Seen by both eyes

Sneaking up

Prey can stay hidden from predators using **camouflage**. Predators also need to stay hidden so that their prey does not see them until it is too late. Many forms of camouflage use spots or stripes to

break up the shape

of the animal and make it harder to spot them. From a distance, potential prey might not see the tiger lurking in the grass. Predators will normally target young, old or injured prey. When it is fleeing a predator such as a cheetah, a gazelle may leap high in the air to display its fitness in the hope that the predator will look elsewhere for its meal. This behaviour is called **stotting**, or **pronking**.

TRY THIS

Some animals disguise themselves by pretending to be something else. Can you spot the animals hiding in plain view in these images?

1. Stick insects are shaped like twigs and leaves.

2. Octopuses can change their colour in order to blend in with their surroundings. Here one has disguised itself as a piece of coral.

3. This mossy leaf-tailed gecko is coloured like the bark and moss of a tree.

Taking flight

Animals such as birds, bats
and insects fly through
the air using wings.

The bend in the middle of the wing is the bird's wrist.

The upper arm is short and thick, for powering the wing beat: this part is hidden on most birds.

The last joint of the wing is like a hand, but it has only one finger bone. This holds all the long primary feathers used for flying.

On the wing

A bird's wings are its front legs covered in feathers. Birds need to be as light as possible to stay in the sky. To save weight, their bones are

hollow.

20

In the 19th century, German engineer **Otto Lilienthal** studied the flight of birds and designed the first glider. To make your own glider, you'll need eight straws, tissue paper and sticky tape.

- Join three straws by pushing the end of one inside another by a couple of centimetres. Make another set of three straws and one of two.
- Bend the top of one of the three-straws and join it to the other three-straws to make a 'V'. Bend the corners of the two-straws and join it to the V to make a triangular frame.
- Place the frame on a sheet of tissue paper and wrap the paper tightly around both sides of the frame. Tape the paper in place, keeping it as tight as possible. **Now fly your glider**.

Wings can rotate to different angles, giving the bird superb control

Acrobats in the sky

Hummingbirds have rotating wings, which allow them to fly **forwards, backwards, sideways or straight up.** They can also hover perfectly still in the same place as they drink the sweet nectar from flowers.

Gliders

The flying squirrel does not use powered flight. Instead, it glides from tree to tree using **flaps between its front and rear legs.**

"Who are you? and you? and you?"

Microorganisms

Microorganisms, or microbes, are tiny life forms that are too small to see with the naked eye. Each microbe is made of just a single cell.

Bacteria

Measuring just a few millionths of a metre across, single-celled bacteria are the **most common form of life**. There are more bacteria on Earth than there are stars in the Universe. Bacteria have been found living 1,000 metres deep under Antarctic ice and 10,000 metres high in Earth's atmosphere. Our bodies contain

trillions of bacteria,

many of which live in our guts and help us to digest our food.

Slime mould

Slime moulds are single-celled microbes that spend most of their lives on their own, but come together in their hundreds of thousands when food is scarce to form a **slug-like blob** that crawls along the ground at about 1 mm per hour devouring food particles as it goes.

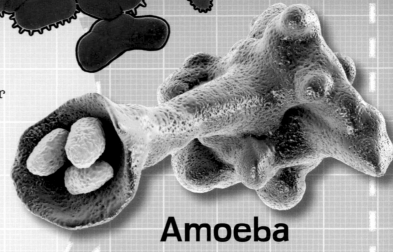

Amoeba

Amoeba are single-celled creatures called **protozoans** that move by **changing their body shapes**. They prey on other microorganisms by trapping them inside their bodies.

TRY THIS

Bacteria reproduce very quickly. You can grow your own bacteria in a petri dish filled with agar (a form of gelatine that you can buy in health food shops). To see what bacteria there may be around your house, swab a cotton bud along the surface of your kitchen sink. Rub the bud gently over the agar, then put the lid on to seal the dish and leave it in a warm place for three days. Make a drawing of how the dish looks when you return, then dispose of it safely by wrapping it in newspaper. Try other dishes with swabs from underneath your finger or toe nails. **How do they compare?**

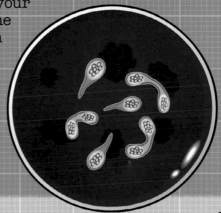

Getting smart

Some animals have evolved to be smart. A big brain takes a lot of energy to maintain, but it allows the animals to solve tricky problems.

Amazing trunks

An elephant's trunk is a **mass of muscle**. The trunk is powerful enough to knock down trees, but it is also **incredibly sensitive** and can pick up a single blade of grass. It also has an **incredible sense of smell**. Elephants use their trunks to explore the world around them, as humans would use their hands. Elephants have big brains to make sense of the information they find.

Elephants greet each other using their trunks.

Smart arms

The clever octopus uses its **flexible arms** to solve problems. In tests, octopuses have learned how to unscrew jars to get at food inside them.

Nut crackers

Crows in Japan have worked out a clever way to crack nuts with a little help from humans. The crows drop their nuts on a pedestrian crossing and **wait at the side of the road** while cars drive over the nuts to crush them. When the crossing turns green, the crows walk out into the road to eat the nuts.

TRY THIS

Look at the image below for just two seconds, then cover it up and try to remember exactly where each number is. **Did you get it right?** Scientists were amazed to discover that chimpanzees can do this task without error! Chimpanzees have the ability to remember details of an image they have only seen very briefly. This is known as eidetic, or photographic, memory.

6   1
  4
    5   9
  7
2   8

Extinct

Asteroid strike

Sometimes extinctions are caused by a sudden change in conditions. One of these occurred **66 million years ago** after an asteroid about

15 km across

struck Earth. The impact threw clouds of dust high into the atmosphere, where it is thought to have blocked out the Sun for several months. About **three quarters of all species** on Earth were made extinct by the strike, including all the large-bodied dinosaurs.

Crater is 180 km wide

The impact crater from the asteroid was discovered in 1978 buried underneath the Yucatán Peninsula in Mexico.

The fossil record

We know about extinct species through the remains of plants or animals that have been preserved in rocks as fossils, such as this ammonite, which lived about 100 million years ago.

Stuck in time

This 74-million-year-old fossil of a Velociraptor and a Protoceratops was discovered in 2006 in the Gobi Desert. It shows the two dinosaurs engaged in a fight. The Velociraptor appears to have been trying to kill the Protoceratops when they were both

buried in sand
during a landslide.

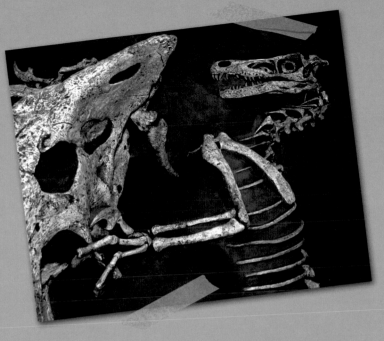

This mosquito was trapped in sticky tree resin more than 40 million years ago. Over time, the resin has hardened into amber,

preserving the body
of the insect inside.

Human impact

By examining the fossil record, scientists have worked out that, before humans evolved, an average of one species per million went extinct each year. That rate has increased to more than **100 species per million per year** due to habitat destruction and climate change caused by humans. New nature reserves, both on land and in the oceans, are needed to slow down this rate. Today, fewer than **100 Sumatran rhinoceroses** remain. Much of the rainforest in which they live has been destroyed, and scientists fear that the species will soon become extinct.

Quiz

1 This cladogram shows the common ancestors for different groups of reptile and bird.

     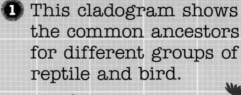

Turtles **Tuataras** **Snakes** **Lizards** **Crocodiles** **Dinosaurs** **Birds**

Early amniote

a Which group is the **closest relative** to the dinosaurs?

b Which group is **most distantly related** to all the others?

c Are snakes more closely related to **lizards** or **tuataras**?

2 **Which gas**, absorbed by the leaves of plants, is needed for photosynthesis?

28

3 The process of photosynthesis releases **which gas** into the atmosphere?

4 What is the name for a group of **similar organisms** that reproduce with one another?

5 This hummingbird is feeding on a **flower's nectar**. What is the name of the **powdery substance** that the bird will carry to another flower to fertilise it?

6 Which of the following animals is not classed as a vertebrate?

7 What is the name of the **group of animals** that produce milk to feed their young?

a) Spider

b) Lizard

c) Shark

8 This **nymph** (right) is the
underwater larva
of **which insect?**
a) Dragonfly
b) Butterfly
c) Moth

9 A **fish's gills** take in
which substance that is
dissolved
in water?
a) Nitrogen
b) Carbon dioxide
c) Oxygen

11 Large dinosaurs became
extinct **66 million years ago**
after which dramatic event?

10 Which is the most **common
form of life** on Earth?
a) Fungi
b) Bacteria
c) Mammals

12 The body of this scorpion
(left) **has been preserved** in
amber.
Amber is made of
which substance?
a) Magma from
a volcano
b) The saliva
of animals
c) Fossilised
tree resin

Glossary

Bacteria
Single-celled organisms that are found all over the planet.

Camouflage
The shape or colouring of an animal that allows it to hide, either by making it hard to see or by disguising it as something else.

Cladogram
A diagram that shows the last common ancestors of different species or groups of species.

Coral
A stony substance made of the skeletons of dead animals, which forms large reefs in tropical oceans.

Evolution
The process by which new species develop over time through natural selection.

Exoskeleton
The hard protective covering of animals such as insects and spiders.

Extinction
The disappearance of a species from Earth when the last of its members dies.

Fossil
The remains of an organism that have been preserved in rock or amber.

Larva
The young form of an insect, which may look very different from the adult form.

Microbe
Also called a microorganism, a single-celled organism that is usually too small to be seen with the naked eye.

Organism
An individual plant, animal or microbe.

Photosynthesis
The process by which plants and algae use the energy of the Sun to produce the substances they need to grow. It releases oxygen into the air.

Pollination
The fertilisation of a flowering plant's egg cells by sperm cells found in pollen. The pollen is usually carried from one flower to another so that plants are fertilised by the pollen of different plants of the same species.

Pupa
A stage in the life cycle of an insect in which it is stationary and changing its body. In butterflies and moths, this stage is also called a chrysalis.

Respiration
A process in all organisms in which energy is released from sugars. It also releases carbon dioxide into the air.

Species
A group of similar organisms that reproduce with one another to produce fertile offspring.

Vertebrate
An animal that has a backbone.

Index

Answers

1. a) Birds b) Turtles c) Lizards
2. Carbon dioxide
3. Oxygen
4. Species
5. Pollen
6. a) Spider
7. Mammals
8. a) Dragonfly
9. c) Oxygen
10. b) Bacteria
11. An asteroid struck Earth
12. c) Fossilised tree resin

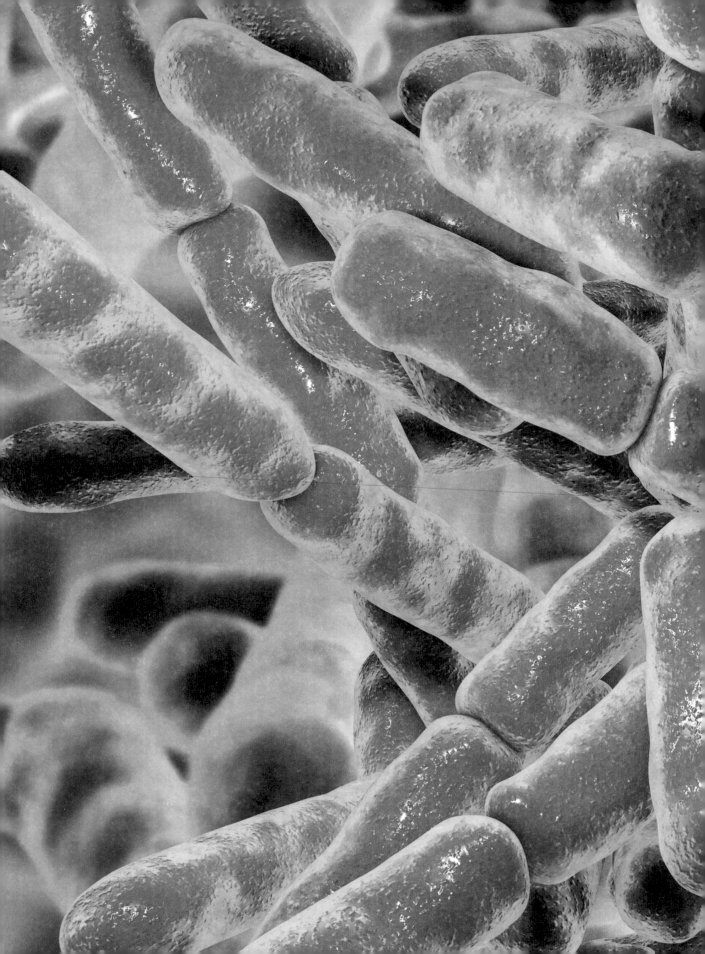